SCHIRMER'S LIBRARY
OF MUSICAL CLASSICS

LUDWIG VAN BEETHOVEN

Concerto No. 1

For the Piano

Provided with Fingering, and with a
Complete Arrangement, for Piano,
of the Orchestral Accompaniment

by

FRANZ KULLAK

The Introduction and Notes
translated from the German

by

DR. THEODORE BAKER

G. SCHIRMER, Inc.

DISTRIBUTED BY

HAL•LEONARD
CORPORATION

7777 W. BLUEMOUND RD. P.O.BOX 13819 MILWAUKEE, WI 53213

Notes to Beethoven's Concerto in C major

By FRANZ KULLAK

Ludwig van Beethoven's Concerto in C major, which he himself styled "Grand Concert," was published as op. 15 in March, 1801, by T. Mollo & Co., in Vienna. Its opus-number renders it, *for us*, the first of the series. In point of fact, however, and according to the composer's own statement in a letter to Breitkopf & Härtel of April 22, 1802 [Thayer: II, 129], it was written later than the B♭-major Concerto (No. 2), which was published as op. 19, towards the end of 1801, by Hoffmeister & Co.

More recently, this statement has not only been confirmed from Beethoven's Sketch-books by G. Nottebohm,[*] but the periods of composition, and the date of the first performance of at least one of these Concertos, have been approximately established by the same writer ; though these times are not yet fixed beyond cavil. Nottebohm has shown :

(1) That the B♭-major Concerto can hardly have been finished before the middle of 1794.[†]

(2) It must have been finished, at latest, by March 29, 1795 ; because on that date, to the best of our knowledge, Beethoven played in public for the first time in Vienna a concerto of his own composition, which cannot possibly have been a still earlier unpublished one, written in his twelfth year.

(3) That the C-major Concerto must have been finished before July, 1798.

(4) That it is improbable that the latter Concerto was completed as early as March 29, 1795 ; and, even if it had been, it seems probable that the composer would have first performed the composition first completed.

To this last reason we cannot subscribe quite unconditionally ; for what should have prevented the composer from choosing, for his first public appearance, the concerto which he thought to be the grander or more beautiful, and with which he promised himself the greater success ?

Neither do we feel inclined to belittle the musical credibility of a personal friend, physician, and biographer of the composer with regard to an anecdote which, if authentic, would still further narrow down the period of the completion and first performance of the C-major Concerto. It is this : Wegeler (in "Biogr. Notizen über L. van B.," Coblenz, 1838 [Thayer : I, 294]) narrates that Beethoven, while laboring under quite severe indisposition, wrote the Rondo "of his First Concerto (C major) only on the afternoon of the second day previous to its performance. . . . In the anteroom were sitting four copyists, to whom he gave the single sheets as fast as he finished them. . . . At the first rehearsal, which took place next day in Beethoven's room, the piano was found to be a semitone too low for the wind-instruments ; Beethoven immediately let them tune to the pitch of *b♭*[*] instead of *a*, and played his part in C♯ major."

Nottebohm assumes, that Wegeler "simply mistook one concerto for the other." But Wegeler was, at least, sufficiently musical to be able to set words to compositions by Beethoven. And his remark is of peculiar interest

---

[*] In the Leipzig "Musikalisches Wochenblatt" of Nov. 26, 1875 ; Vol. VI, No. 48.

[†] It is curious that the imitative passages written (in another ink) for his lessons with Albrechtsberger begin on the third page of the double sheet containing the sketches for the B♭-major Concerto, and yet were supposedly written earlier than the latter. To be sure, this third page might originally have been the first.

[*] To the *b♭* of his piano ! The semitonic difference was probably not precise, and the wind-players could easily reconcile slight fluctuations. Or does Nottebohm hold the speedy transposition of an entire concerto (or of only the Rondo) to be almost incredible ? The transposition (*i.e.*, of the wind-parts [TRANSLATOR'S NOTE]) was implied, rather than real. At such a rehearsal, precision of execution was not the main object. Beethoven's marked aversion to transposed music in general (see Schindler, II, 166-7) cannot be urged as an argument in such a case of necessity. The large number of orchestral players said to have been present at the performance of the C-major Concerto (11 wind-players, besides the drummer ; the B♭-major Concerto requires only 7 wind-players) is more calculated to excite suspicion. But Beethoven was then living as the guest of a Prince ! (Karl Lichnowsky.—Wegeler, p. 28 ; Thayer : I, 204). But also compare, concerning Beethoven's dwellings at that time, Thayer : II, 103 (not without the addendum, III, 510), whereby Wegeler's statement touching his place of residence is called in question. Moreover, some 16 or 17 years later, Beethoven transposed the Horn Sonata, op. 17, without preparation, from F major to F♯. (Nohl, in "Beethoven nach den Schilderungen seiner Zeitgenossen," p. 145 ; after a communication from Starke.)

to us, as connecting the performance of a Beethoven Concerto with Wegeler's brief stay in Vienna (from the end of 1794 to the middle of 1796). Furthermore, as Beethoven himself went on tours early in 1796 (in Prague on Feb. 19; from June 21 to 28—or later—in Berlin), Wegeler could have had in mind, among public performances of the piano-concertos towards the end of this period (*i.e.*, of those known to us), only those given on Dec. 18, 1795, or Jan. 8, 1796. Nottebohm does not mention the latter; consequently, he leaves it undecided whether it was the C-major Concerto which Beethoven played on Dec. 18, 1795; only this date appears to him too early to justify Beethoven's expression, "a concerto finished more recently."* Still, if the Wegeler anecdote refers to the C-major Concerto, the B♭ major Concerto might, after all, have been completed some time (as much as nine months) before the performance of March 29, 1795, and Beethoven would have had time, even after this, to begin on a new concerto and finish it by Dec. 16, 1795,† or Jan. 6, 1796.‡ So indefatigable a spirit might well have attained the larger development within a year and a half.

To add to the existing confusion, Tomaschek, who heard both of Beethoven's concertos at Prague in 1798, that in C major being the first, narrates as follows: "He [Beethoven] played this time the Concerto in B♭ major, composed after coming to Prague" (!). Nottebohm assumes that this may have been the posthumous Rondo in B♭ major, written "doubtless prior to 1800." But Tomaschek, who was possibly acquainted with this circumstance only through hearsay, may also have "mistaken one concerto for the other," taking the one last played to be the one last composed!

We cannot deny that two reasons, in particular, argue against Wegeler's assumption:

(1) The considerable length of the Rondo to the C-major Concerto.

(2) The circumstance, that in the autograph of the B♭-major Concerto, the pianoforte-part, save a few sketches, is wanting; whereas, this part, in the score of the C-major Concerto, is extant in an almost complete form, even for the Rondo.*

We must, of course, leave the decision of all these questions to historical research. From its style, we should relegate the composition of the B♭-major Concerto to the time of the E♭ Trio, op. 1, and that of the C-major Concerto to about the time of the C-major Sonata, op. 2, No. 3.

Of the other notices touching the performance of the C-major Concerto, we mention Carl Czerny's (in "Kunst des Vortrags," p. 105), according to which " Beethoven himself (1801) played this First Concerto in the Kärnthnerthor Theatre;" also Schindler's more precise statement (" Beethoven," Third Ed., p. 57): " The first performance of this work, given by the composer himself, took place in the spring of 1800 at the Kärnthnerthor Theatre, with great applause." Both these notices are inexact, as the following list, arranged to give a more convenient general view, will show. The appended remarks, from programs or criticisms, are copied from Nottebohm and Thayer.

LIST OF CONCERTS
AT WHICH BEETHOVEN PERFORMED A PIANO-FORTE-CONCERTO.
VIENNA.
Sunday, March 29, 1795. [Th.: I, 294.]
Concert in the Burgtheater, for the benefit of the widows of the Society of Musicians [*Tonkünstlergesellschaft*].

" . . . a new concerto, . . . and of his own composition.—. . . an entirely new concerto, written by himself." . . . [No key.] (N.)

---

* More exactly: "a concerto finished, *it is true*, more recently," for Beethoven says it in an apologetic tone. (When he wrote this letter, he had already finished the Third, and greater, Concerto.)

† True, in the meantime the 12 Minuets and the 12 German Dances for orchestra, which must have been finished by Nov. 22, 1795, were composed [Th.: I, 297; also Nottebohm: "Them. Catalogue," Second Ed., 1868, p. 136]. But he is said to have written out the Rondo in one day!

‡ The fact that preliminary work for a cadenza to the B♭ Concerto is found on one and the same sheet with sketches for the Rondo of the Concerto in C (Nottebohm: "Mus. Wochenblatt") might be taken as evidence to bring the Concertos nearer together in point of time.

* Three different shades of ink! Of the piano-part of the Rondo only detached passages (*e.g.*, for one hand alone) appear to have been written out originally; ditto the entry of the 1st violins, in the first Tutti. More filled in later. Finally, innumerable corrections were made, perhaps after the first performance! The whole a perfect chaos. On the contrary, the score of the B♭ Concerto might be termed comparatively orderly and clean; though in the first movement it likewise exhibits supplementary corrections and cuts in a very pale ink, which, however, were not followed in publication. To prevent useless researches, we add that, so far as we were able to make out (despite the firm stitching; each movement is stitched together as a separate book), the Rondos of both concertos are written, in the main, on pairs of double sheets laid one within the other; and that a separate double sheet, or a single sheet, occurs only by way of exception in either book.

Friday, December 18, 1795. [Th.: II, 298.]
Grand Musical Academy [Concert] by Haydn.
" . . . at which Herr v. B. will play
a Concerto of his own composition on
the Forte-Piano." [No key.]

(Sojourn in Prague during the Christmas
holidays of 1795. [Th.: II, 6; here an
"Academy" is also spoken of, which B. is
said to have given at Prague in 1795].)

Friday, January 8, 1796. [Th.: II, 5.]
Concert of Signora Bolla.
B. plays a concerto (Haydn conducting).
[No key.]

1796: journey to Prague (prior to Feb.
19), and to Berlin, where B. plays (improvises)
at the Singacademie, June 21 and 28. [Th.:
II, 13.]

PRAGUE.

1798. [Th.: II, 29 and 30.]
B. plays the Concertos in C major and B♭
major.

VIENNA.

October 27, 1798. [Th.: II, 32.]
Concert in Schikaneder's theatre in the
Staremberg "Freihaus auf der Wieden."
B. plays "a pianoforte-concerto of his
own composition" (according to Thay-
er). [No key.]

Wednesday, April 2, 1800. [Th.: II, 97.]
Grand Musical Academy in the Imperial
Royal National Court Theatre "nächst
der Burg" [near the castle].
Program: A grand Concerto for the
Pianoforte, played and composed by
Herrn Ludwig van Beethoven.
(A symphony by Beethoven, also given on
the same program, is styled "new.")
Criticism (in the Leipzig "Allgem. Mus.
Zeitung"): " . . . a new con-
certo, . . . which contains many
beauties, especially the last two move-
ments." [No key.]

Tuesday, April 5, 1803. [Th.: II, 222.]
Concert in the Imp. R. Chartered Theater
an der Wien.
Criticism ("Zeitung f. d. elegante Welt"):
" . . . Less successful [hence,
new !] was the following Concerto in
C minor,* which Herr v. B., otherwise

---

* The Autograph bears, in the composer's handwriting, the
title:
Concerto 1800 Da L. v. Beethoven.
Of the pianoforte-part, only fragments are contained in this auto-

---

known as an excellent pianist, also
did not perform to the full satisfaction
of the audience."

SOURCES CONSULTED FOR THE C-MAJOR CONCERTO.

Our reading of the Soli results from a
collation of the Breitkopf & Härtel edition
(Complete Edition) with the Autograph of the
score,* on the one hand, and, on the other,
with an edition published by T. Mollo (No.
1107);† and we have accepted only such readings, in the principal text, as are guaranteed
either by Mollo or the Autograph. Supplementary signs (slurs, staccato) introduced by
us into the principal text, are given in lighter
characters; but all further emendations are
relegated to the Notes.

As for the above-mentioned edition by
T. Mollo, it is merely a later edition of the
original publication by T. Mollo & Comp.
(No. 153).‡ On comparing the Soli of both
these editions, measure by measure, we found
no traces whatever of supplementary corrections. Between these two editions doubtless
came the one designated by Nottebohm (Them.
Catalogue: Second Edition, 1868) as No. 953,§
published by T. Mollo & Comp.

---

graph. In 1803 Beethoven played, as Ries narrates (Th.: II, 224),
"almost the entire principal part from memory alone," Ries
having to turn the *blank pages* for him. Thayer "considers the
conjecture justifiable," that the composition of this Concerto
dates only from the summer of that year (Th.: II, 105). Had it
been finished as early as March, we should, indeed, have reason
to be surprised that the composer did not bring about its performance on April 2, 1800.

* In the Royal Library, Berlin.

† Also in the Royal Library. The full title of this "oblong"
edition reads: "*Grand Concert pour le Forte-Piano avec deux
Violons, deux Alto, Basse et Violoncelle, deux Flûtes,*[1] *deux Oboë,
deux Clarinettes, deux Bassons,*[2] *deux Trompettes, et Timballes
composé et dédié À Son Altesse Madame la Princesse Odescalchi
née Comtesse Keglevics par Louis van Beethoven Œuvre 15. No.
1107.* [to the right] . . . . . . [to the left] *f* [illegible] *à Vienne
chez T. Mollo.*" Inside: "M. 1107."

[1] More correctly, "*Une Flûte.*"

[2] "*Deux Cors*" were left out.

‡ Also in the Royal Library. The title, otherwise precisely
similar, bears the following signature:

153.   à Vienne chez T. Mollo et Comp.   *f* 4,; 30.
*Leipzig au Comptoir d'Industrie
Franckfort chez Gayl et Hedler.*

Inside, only "153."

§ We have seen a later reprint of Beethoven's Violin-Sonata,
op. 23 (originally united with op. 24, but afterwards separated;
published by Mollo & Co.), in which the earlier plate-number 173
(inside) had very evidently been altered into 973. The original
edition of op. 15 (T. Mollo & Comp.) appeared in 1801. In 1803 the
firm-name was still "T. Mollo & Comp." (Nottebohm: "Them.
Cat.," V, p. 138); in Sept. 1808 (Nott., p. 180), it was "T. Mollo"
(No. 1487). But we think it doubtful whether this last register
[running number of publication] is the original one. We have
seen a sonata by Beethoven, op. 81 ("Les Adieux"), publ. by T.
Mollo with the register 1375, which cannot well have been written
before 1810. Consequently, we should assume the year 1808 as the
approximate date of the T. Mollo edition No. 1107 of our concerto
(the edition we mentioned first).

Furthermore, we consulted another edition, published by N. Simrock as No. 187,* carefully comparing the soli with those of the Mollo edition. From the striking agreement of these two editions, which extends even to errors of engraving, we arrived at the conviction, that either Mollo's edition served as a model for Simrock, or that both are to be referred to a common source.

Regarding the external appearance of these old prints, it will be of interest to learn that in the Mollo edition the Tutti are still represented in the most old-fashioned style by figured basses only, with the same large note-heads and expression-marks as the Soli. During the Tutti, the right hand has rests. The word "tutti" occurs but once; "solo" not at all. The Simrock edition retains the figured basses, but adds in many places small notes for the right hand, thus giving the

player a choice of three different modes of performance (see title-page): With stringed instruments only [in this case the extra viola is absolutely necessary], with a few wind-instruments, or with full orchestra.

Our arrangement of the orchestral part follows the score published by Breitkopf & Härtel, compared with the Autograph. Slurs and staccato-marks, given very sparingly in the latter, were added by us in lighter characters. We write the staccato-marks uniformly throughout. Whereas the Autograph has dots only by way of exception, as if by accident (except in the form ⌒....⌒), Mollo exhibits quite a medley of dots and pointed dashes. In the very first *marcato*, M. gives dashes! In his edition, the staccato-dashes occurring below the note-heads, with the point downward (♩), would almost seem to indicate corrections made at first hand. But, for writing the appoggiaturas, we retained the notation of the composer (and of the Simrock edition). Mollo, for the short appoggiatura, has ♪; in Largo also ♪. In accordance with modern practice, we invariably write accidentals altering the *lowest* note of a turn, *below* the turn-sign ∾.

F. K.

BERLIN, Summer of 1881.

---

* The title of this edition, surrounded by a wreath, reads: "*Grand | Concert | pour le Piano-Forte | avec accompagnement de toutes les parties d'orchestre | (on peut aussi l'exécuter à 6 parties) | composé par | L. van Beethoven. | Œuvre 15 | Prix 10. Francs. | A Paris aux adresses ordinaires. | À Bonn chez N. Simrock |*"
(Outside of the wreath :)
No. 187.   Pr. 4¾ Fl.
                  Pr. Fr. 10.
Orchestral parts also. This edition was doubtless published during the composer's lifetime. Below the former owner's name is written, in ink, the date 1820. Time of publication, however, was probably prior to 1804.

First Concerto.

Dedicated to Princess Odescalchi, *née* Countess Keglevics.

L. van BEETHOVEN, Op. 15.

(1) The metronome-mark ♩=88 (i.e., ♩=176), given by Czerny in the "Kunst des Vortrags" (Art of Interpreting: Supplement to the great Pianoforte-Method, op. 500), corresponds neither with the prescribed tempo and the four-four time, nor with the festive character of the movement.

(2) writes the arranger of the Tutti in the Haslinger Edition (№ 7075; publ. about 1837) directly in the text.

(3) Flute, Oboes, Clarinets, Bassoons, Horns, Trumpets, Timp. and String-quartet (-quintet).

(1) Breitkopf & Härtel's score gives ♮.— Autograph not quite plain, but probably ♭ or ♭♮. In that case, to be sure, the ♮ in the Autograph for Violins I and II, in the next measure, appears superfluous.

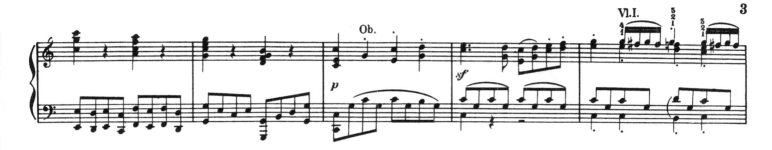

(1) Czerny adds "*p*."

15355

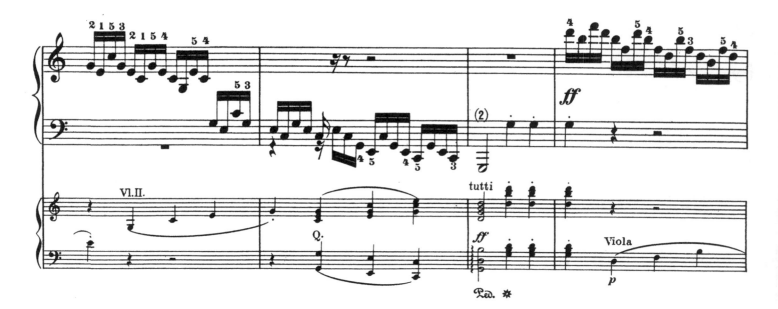

(1) In the autograph (of the score) these basses are also written in the piano-part, and should, therefore, probably be played by it. (In the score they are also given to the 1st bassoon and the drum). Also *c.f.* our note to the C-minor Concerto, p. 60.

(2) Mollo's thorough-bass figuring is   ; this is incorrect, as the score shows.

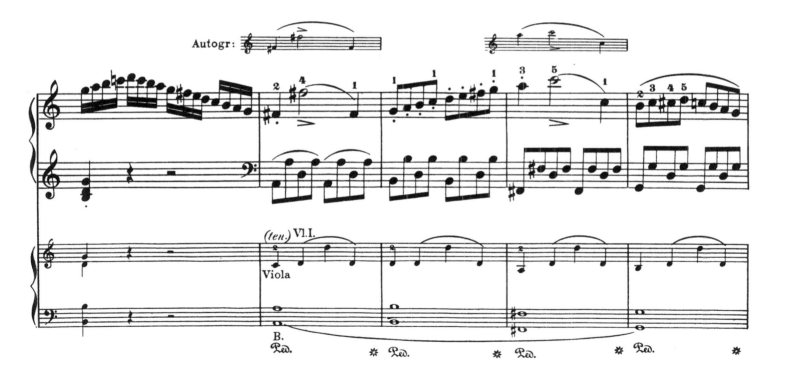

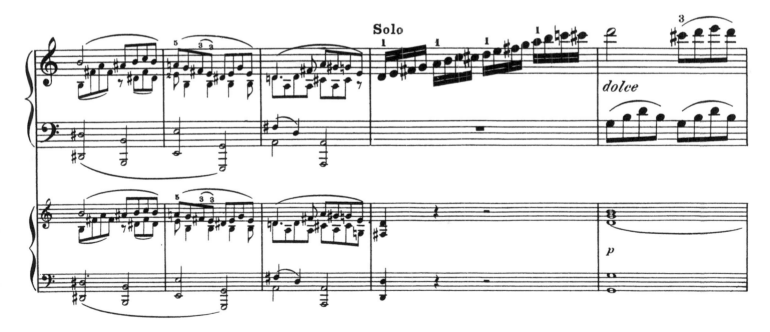

Br. & H., and Autogr., only 𝄢

(1) Not given in the Autograph. Instead, in lieu of dots, "staccato" is written in the third beat.

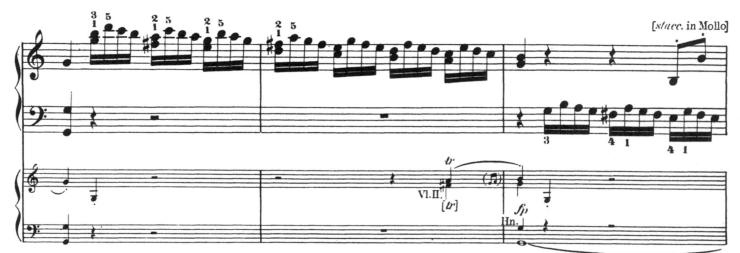

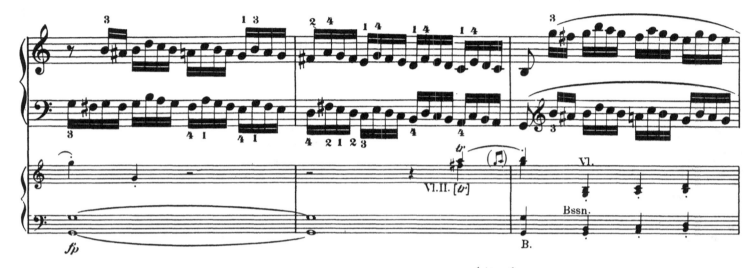

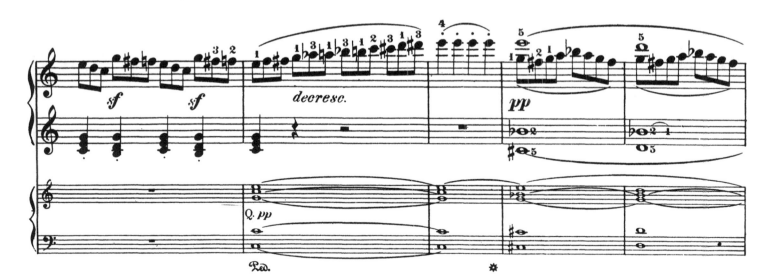

(1) A slur from *c* to *b*, both in Mollo and Autograph, was probably left there accidentally.

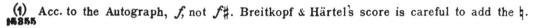

(1) Acc. to the Autograph, *f*, not *f♯*. Breitkopf & Härtel's score is careful to add the ♮.

(1) Probably incorrect. The Autograph reads as above.

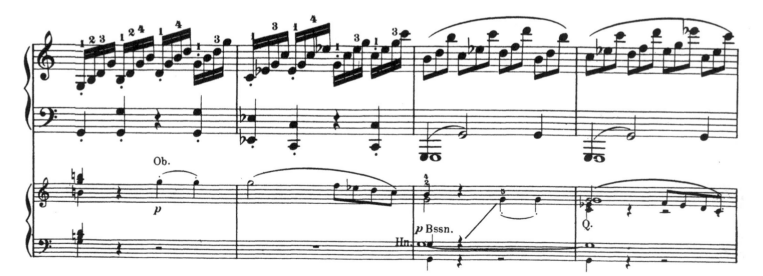

(1) Mollo has *f*, probably a mere oversight.

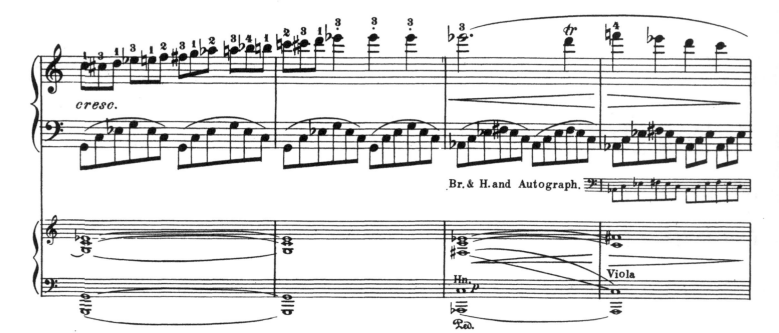

(1) This bass is lacking in the Autograph (also in Br. & H.). Was it not merely forgotten by the composer?

(1) In the Autograph this *pp* comes after the bar.

(2) "Senza sordino", *with Pedal*; "Con sordino", *without Pedal* (✳). It would seem entirely proper to modify the use of the pedal in conformity with the requirements of modern pianos; here, for instance, to take the pedal anew with each new harmony.

(3) Acc. to Mollo, arpeggio in both hands. Beethoven, who wrote, in his autographs, the arpeggio-mark as a slanting line (𝄐), had stricken out the left-hand chords so marked, and supplied non-arpeggio'd chords. Breitkopf & Härtel also follow this reading.

(4) On this *glissando* Czerny remarks: "The reëntry into the principal theme is again effected by an octave-slide with two fingers (as in the solo Sonata, Op. 53), and small hands may, therefore, take it as a simple *glissando* scale, in which case it should be prolonged to the octave below, with increased swiftness". It would then be played about as follows:

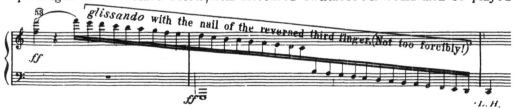

It might be less in keeping with the style (anachronism!), but possibly more practical, to prolong the *glissando* an octave further yet. But one might just as well execute the original reading (omitting the contra *G*) with both hands as an ordinary scale, or (which, to be sure, is harder) as a *glissando*.

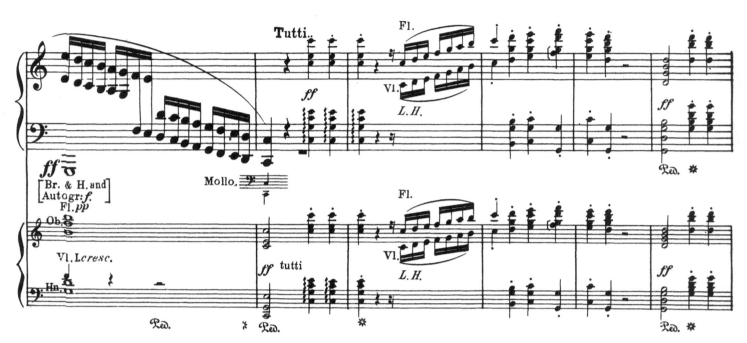

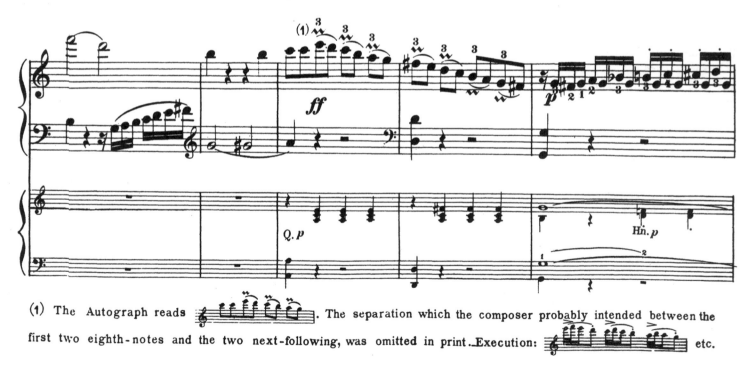

(1) The Autograph reads . The separation which the composer probably intended between the first two eighth-notes and the two next-following, was omitted in print. Execution: etc.

(1) Instead of this quarter-note, the Autograph has a quarter-rest ( ). Is this not a mere oversight? (However, Breitkopf & Härtel's score follows the Autograph.)

Mollo (by an oversight?) only

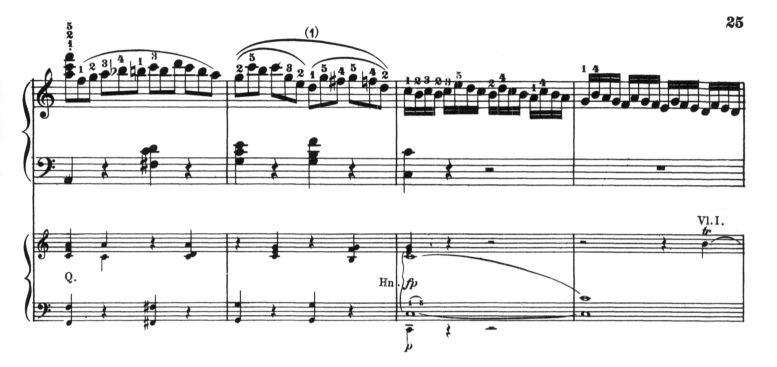

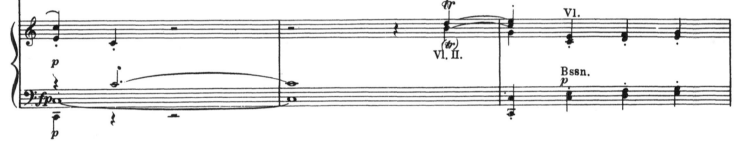

(1) The upper slur acc. to Mollo.

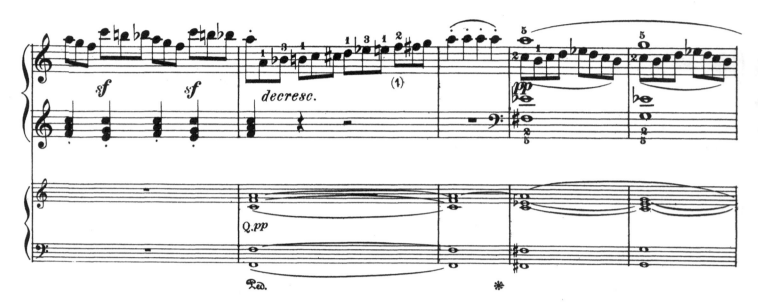

(1) So in Mollo and the Autograph. Breitkopf & Härtel's emendation: ; ditto in Haslinger (N⁰ **7075**). For

the rest, the evident harshness of the original might be softened, within the triplet, as follows:

(2) The *sf* of the Autograph is omitted in Mollo, who writes an *f* instead at the beginning of the next measure. At this point, on the other hand, the Autograph writes *cresc.*, which comes in Mollo two measures earlier. Our reading is a combination from both sources, following (like Br. & H.) the parallel passage on p. **12**.

(1) Breitkopf & Härtel .(T. Haslinger ditto.)

15855

(1) Timpani, acc to. Br. & H.'s score ♯♯♯ Autograph omits the 𝄢 ♯♯, probably by oversight, and likewise the 𝆑, which appears only in the 1st violin-part.
(2) For the 3 Cadenzas by Beethoven, see Appendix.

15355

Largo. (M. M. ♩=58, following Czerny, perhaps slightly more animated.)

After B.& H. and the Autogr:

(1) ₵ (not C), acc. to the Autograph, Mollo, and Czerny, who adds: "This *Largo* is *alla breve*, and therefore to be taken as a tranquil *Andante*." (However, Schindler opposes such a conception of *alla breve* time ["Beethoven", Third Ed. II, 245].)

(2) The ornament is omitted in the Autograph, and by Br. & H.

(3) Clarinets, Bassoons, Horns and **String-quartet.**

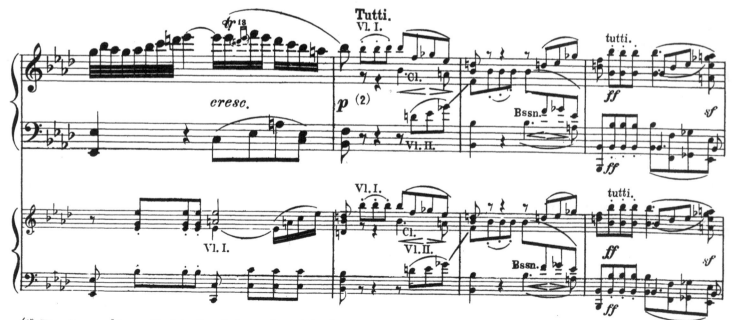

(1) The lower *d* is omitted in the Autograph and by Br. & H.
(2) Mollo gives *p*.

(1) Neither the Autograph nor Br. & H. give the embellishment.

(2) Mollo has ![notes] (with large note-heads). The Autograph also gives the 8 eighth-notes, without figures. In Br. & H. only the first two eighth-notes have large heads. The "*sf. cresc.*" in Mollo is borrowed from the score.

(1) Breitkopf & Härtel add "*p*". Perhaps the composer desired to have the reprise of the theme played more softly [?]. The Autograph throws no light on the matter, as even the last-noted expression-marks, like most of those in this and the final movement, are wanting.

(2) Mollo also gives a long (uncrossed) appoggiatura (♪). The Autograph has [♩], to be executed, acc. to Ph. E. Bach's "Essay", Ch. II, Sect. 2, §§ 7 and 11, as follows: [♩] § 7 says: "All appoggiaturas are more strongly emphasized than the principal note.... The phrasing, when the appoggiatura is followed by a simple unaccented chord-note, is termed a "*lift*" Probable execution: [♩] If Beethoven had wanted it played thus: [♩] he would have written the suspension (appoggiatura) out in large notes of the proper time-value, as in measure 37 of the Largo ([♩]). *Cf.* the § 11 referred to.

(1) Br. & H. give "*pp*"

(1) Mollo gives the upper reading; Br. & H. give the combination:

(2) Autograph: . Single slur; end uncertain. Br. & H. give

(3) Mollo has: "*pp*". The Autograph, in which, however, the preceding "crescendo" is lacking, gives

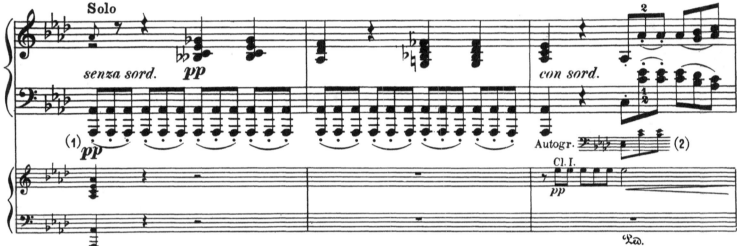

(1) Acc. to the Autograph: ♮. Ditto in Breitkopf & Härtel. In the Autograph, the right-hand chords have the following slurs: (Br. & H. also retain the slurs over the bar). Furthermore, in the Autogr., "senza sordino" begins with the *chords*.

(2) For the notes, Br. & H. follow the Autograph. On the third beat in the next two measures, Mollo has staccato-dashes with the point downward ; if we judge this to be a "correction", and hence conclude that the eye of the proofreader (composer?) dwelt with peculiar care on this passage, Mollo's reading would appear to be final.

(1) Here the ♮ is guaranteed by Mollo, though lacking in the Autograph; we feel unable to accept the emendation

Moreover, Mollo gives only "*sf*" at (×), and "*p cresc.*" at (+), the latter sign not being countermanded later. Our expression-marks follow the Autograph.

(2) The lower reading is from Mollo. For the notes, Br. & H. follow the Autograph. In consideration of the corresponding clarinet solo, the reading in the Autograph would seem to deserve preference.

(1) Divided thus in the Autograph: In Breitkopf & Härtel, the piano-part has a technical emendation of the last group of 32nds to 64ths with a *10* above them. — Without presuming on a critical improvement of the composition, we cannot forbear to observe, touching this measure, that its prolongation into two measures, or at least that of the first half into a whole measure, would have been more in accord with our feeling. At all events, a slight *ritardando* during the passage can hardly be dispensed with, in a thoroughly characteristic interpretation.

(2) The "*senza sordino*" in the Autograph, does not appear until the measure before the last.

Rondo.

Allegro (scherzando) (1) (M.M. ♩ = 132 — 138. — Czerny: ♩ = 72 [i.e., ♩ = 144]).

Solo.

Tutti

(1) *"Allegro scherzando"* say Mollo and (following him) the old editions of Simrock and André. Czerny ditto. The qualification *"scherzando"* is wanting in the Autograph; or, rather, something no longer legible has been erased in this spot.

(2) Czerny adds *"p"*, and, shortly after, *"leggiermente."* "In this theme," he explains, "the pairs of 16th-notes must be isolated by distinctly lifting the second note, which must never be slurred on to the following eighth-note; i.e., rather thus ♫ than thus ♫. The left hand similarly." — We shall not pass judgment on the correctness of this statement. According to Nottebohm ("Beethoveniana," 1872, p. 136) this Concerto was one of the works which Czerny "either heard Beethoven play, or studied under his direction." The fingering which he gives: ♫ is perhaps less likely to promote the required execution, than the following: ♫.

Ries ("Notizen," p. 106) cites the theme of this Rondo as one of the instances in which his teacher, Beethoven, told him to add notes to a composition; here (where?!) "several doubled notes, to render it more brilliant. — Altogether, he interpreted this Rondo with most characteristic expression." — This is, unhappily, too vague to aid us in forming an opinion on Czerny's phrasing.

(3) Orchestration as in First Movement.

(1) Slurs, acc. to the Autograph, consistently thus: etc. Ditto in the parallel passage on p. 54. The first slur in the text would, therefore, appear to have been added later by the composer, and was intended to express, in conjunction with the other, a common bond. This we have indicated by a light slur.

(2) Breitkopf & Härtel's score sets the viola an octave higher (than the attendant violoncello). This was also the original reading in the Autograph, but was later corrected as we now have it. The original viola-part (N⁰ 153) likewise has ; ditto in M., 1107.

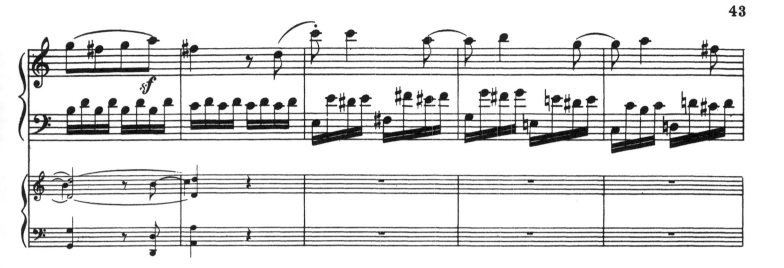

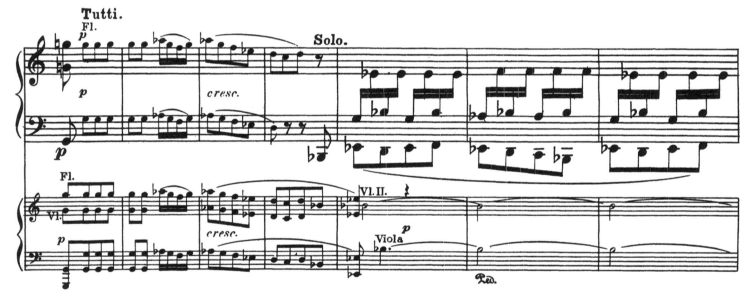

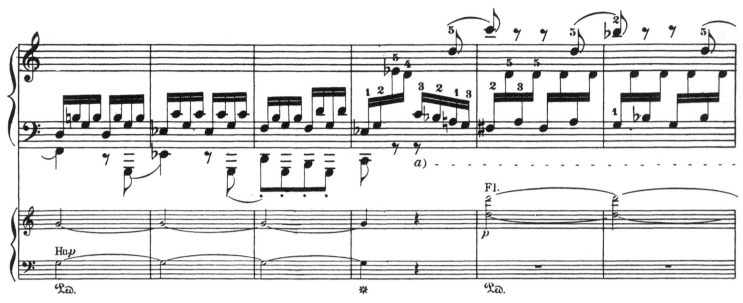

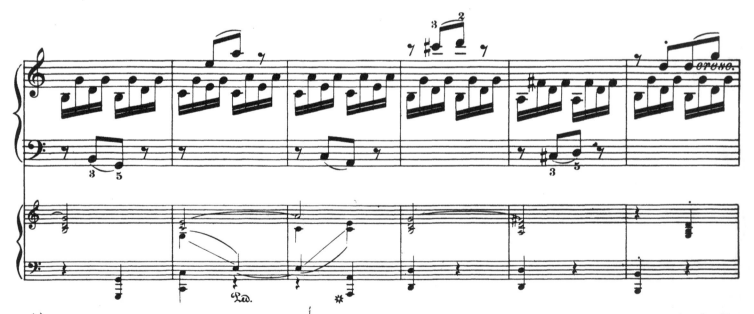

(1) In the Autograph, *g* is lacking, being replaced by an eighth-rest in the upper staff. We must observe, however, that in the parallel passage (p. 58) the corresponding *c* is also found in the Autograph.

(*a*) From here as far as (*b*), it may be easier for many to play the 16th-notes with the left hand.

(1) Acc. to Mollo and the Autograph, "*f*." Emendation in Br. & H.,

(2) Thus Mollo. Rather indistinct in the Autograph. Br. & H. read:

(3) Thus Mollo. — Autogr. (Without expression-marks, which rarely occur in this movement.)

Or, more exactly:
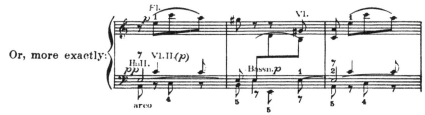

(1) Br. & H. give "d♯"; Mollo and the Autograph (probably an oversight), "e♭."

(2) Autogr.: *(staccato?)*

¹) The Autogr., and Br. & H.'s score, have ♭. Did not the composer merely forget to set a ♮ before ♭? True, the piano-part also gave ♭ 10 measures back, but it began in A-minor. In the parallel passage, 21 measures back, the oboe had [music], whereas before, in the piano-part, we heard [music]

(1) To facilitate execution, these basses may be dropped.

15355

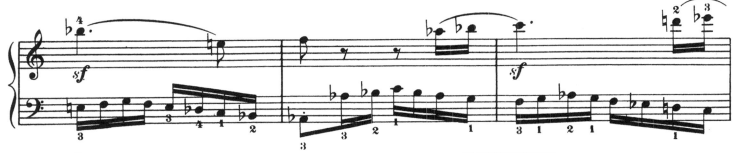

(1) Both in the Autograph and Mollo, although the next eighth-rest is omitted, a quarter-note is written (by mistake?) here.

(2) As given by Mollo and Br. &H. (also see the parallel passage); acc. to the Autograph it reads

(1) Here (probably by mistake) the Autograph gives an isolated slur in the bass part ![notation]. Br. & H.'s score also pays no attention to it, but, instead, adds staccato-dots to the eighth-notes.

(2) Mollo has ![notation]

(a----b) In this passage, too, it might be well to take the 16th-notes with the left hand.

(1) Cadenza acc. to Mollo, Breitkopf & Härtel, Simrock (No. 187), André (No. 2046). T. Haslinger (No. 7075) omits this Cadenza, but gives, at the close of the following solo (in place of the *fermata*), another more brilliant one, which, however, is probably no more traceable to Czerny (not to say, to Beethoven) than the different variants (more difficult readings, employing the higher octaves) accompanying the main text in small notes. (*Cf.* Czerny, "Kunst des Vortrags," Chap. II, 8.) This latter Cadenza, with the variants, is also found in the Peters' score, No. 4241. Although our Cadenza is lacking in the Autograph, the latter contains, in the same place, a direction to leave room for one in the piano-part.

For the rest, if it were permitted, for practical reasons, to add one note to the present Cadenza, we should be

inclined to insert an eighth-note, *c*, just before the trill with which the accompaniment recommences: etc., which would materially promote precision in the reëntry of the orchestra.

(1) (tr)⌒⌒⌒, after Br. & H.'s score.   Autogr:

(2) Br. & H. add "p."   Mollo gives the slurring (only the first time) thus:

(1) Mollo, Br. & H., and others, give "*b*"; we should prefer the (not so very doubtful) *g* in the Autograph.

(1) Here all give *g*.

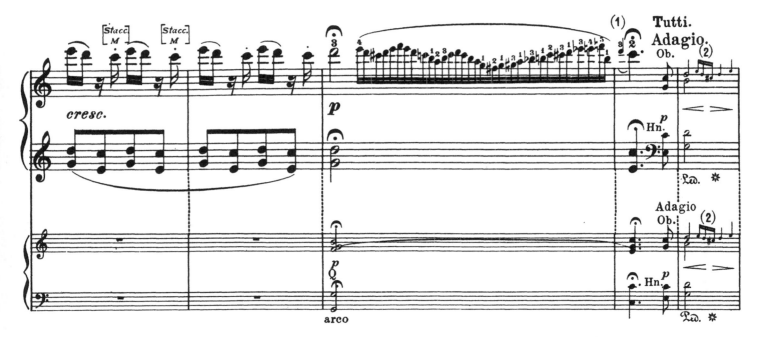

(1) In the already-quoted § 7 of Ph. E. Bach's "Essay" the rule is also given, to slur the appoggiaturas (together with their embellishments) to the following note, "whether a slur be written, or not." Furthermore, acc. to § 11, the long appoggiatura occupies two-thirds of the time-value of a tripartite note (♩.; ♩.). Finally, acc. to § 16, "cases sometimes occur, where the appoggiatura is held longer than usual on account of the expression, and, consequently, fills more than half the time-value of its principal note". (For example: "♪♫♩"; which is in three-four time.) Although the present case (⌢) is not alluded to particularly, we are moved by the above reasons to establish the execution of our last suspension as follows: ♫♩ wherein we allow the fermata about the time-value of a full two-four measure in the already moderated tempo.

(2) The value of the notes acc. to the Autograph.—Br. & H. have ♫♩. In the Autograph, *Adagio* is given only in the 1st oboe part. The following "Tempo I^mo" is wanting in the autogr.

Appendix.

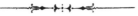

Cadenzas [*]
to the First Movement.

№ 1.

(1) Instead of *"p,"* *"dim."* occurs in a copy (property of the Royal Library, Berlin; formerly, of Prof. Fischhof, Vienna).

[*] These Cadenzas are given, without opus-numbers, among the authentic works in Nottebohm's Thematic Catalogue of Beethoven's compositions (Second Ed., p. 153); according to a note added therein, the autographs are in the possession of Breitkopf & Härtel. Unpublished during the composer's lifetime, they were printed for the first time, to the best of our knowledge, by the above firm. We shall not attempt to decide whether the composer wrote out these Cadenzas for his own use—as a sort of guide for a yet more ornate production—or for the use of others. At all events they bear, in the form hitherto presented, the stamp of incompleteness; No. 1, indeed, is only a fragment. Under these circumstances the assumption is justified, that Beethoven, supposing him to have intended to publish them at all, would previously have revised them. We have, therefore, taken the liberty of presenting these sketches in a form better calculated to appeal to the understanding and appreciation of non-professionals, by inserting expression-marks in smaller print; we have also, while using the original material as far as possible, given them a more finished form by means of additions and abbreviations. Aside from other interesting features, they will always have the advantage of being less at variance with the character of the concerto, than newer creations almost unavoidably are. True, cadenzas were originally intended to afford free scope for novel productions of the performer's subjective fancy, exhibitions of virtuosity (improvisations, if possible). But Beethoven appears, after a time, to-have become sensible of the impropriety of this practice; at least, in his last Concerto (in $E\flat$, 1809), he did away with it.

The first publishers probably intended to print the series of Cadenzas in chronological order. Beethoven's predilection for making the most of the extreme tones of the piano he happened to be using, might afford a clue.— No. 1, probably identical with No. 161 in the auction-catalogue (Thayer, Chronological Catalogue, p. 179), goes up to three-lined $a\flat$ ($a'''\flat$). It seems to have been unsatisfactory to the composer, and remained unfinished.—He begins No. 2 with the same initial motive; this Cadenza reaches a'''.— Finally, No. 3 goes as high as c''''.— Now, as far as we know, these three tones do not occur in Beethoven's piano-works previous to 1804. The C-minor Concerto, published in November, 1804 (Beethoven did not write out the piano-part until after the performance of 1803; doubtless before the middle of July, 1804, for Ries's personal use), has, for the first time, g''' on the principal staff; whereas higher tones (up to c'''') occur in variants. There is, therefore, scarcely a doubt, that our three Cadenzas stand in no connection with the concert-performance mentioned in the Introduction.

On the other hand, it does not seem inconsistent to suppose that No. 3, for instance, may have been employed at some repetition of the C-major Concerto in the years 1807 or 1808; i. e., after the completion of the C-major Concerto and the Violin-concerto.

As early as 1804-5, Ries had twice repeated the C-minor Concerto. While Beethoven was waiting for two years in the vain hope of giving a grand concert ["Academie"] in one of the court theatres (when finally given, on Dec. 22, 1808, he played the G-major Concerto), he had opportunities for other, in part private, performances. At the two Subscription Concerts arranged at Prince Lobkowitz's for his benefit, "a pianoforte-concerto" by him was produced (March, 1807) [Thayer says, it was already the G-major Concerto]. On April 23, 1808, Friedrich Stein played, in the Burgtheater, "one of his [B.'s] concertos" [Th., III, 34]. On Nov. 15, 1808, B. "conducted" a piano-concerto (one of his own?). Doubtless nothing new [Th., III, 52]. To be sure, among these performances may have been included (to April, 1807) the Violin-concerto transformed into a piano-concerto (?), concerning which B. is said to have told Neate, the Englishman, that he had played it himself [Th., III, 376].

For completeness' sake we add, that contra E, which might well have been employed by the composer in the 3rd Cadenza, was inserted by him for the first time in op. 101 (A-major Sonata; played as new, 1816; publ. 1817 [Nottebohm]). The fourth above c'''', i. e., f'''', occurs (except in the Choral Fantasia, which did not appear until 1811) for the first time in the $E\flat$ Trio, op. 70, No. 2 (finished 1808; publ. 1809 [Nottebohm]).

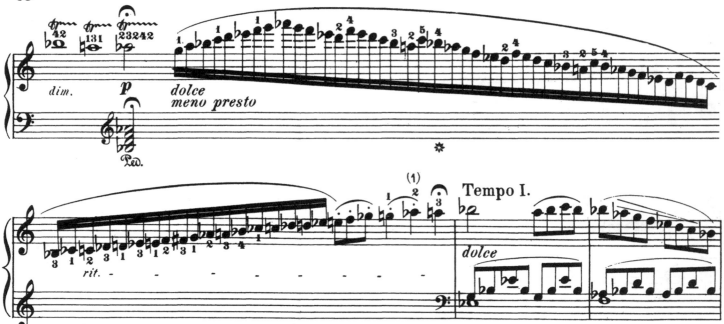

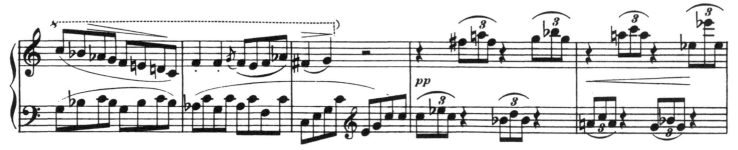

(1) Copy in Royal Library (Fischhof). The bar following is omitted.

(1) "Continuation lacking," says the Breitkopf & Härtel edition. The above-mentioned copy also breaks off here with "down to here;" in the title, the Cadenza is described as "unfinished".—We take the liberty of completing it by adding fragments and motives from the Third Cadenza.

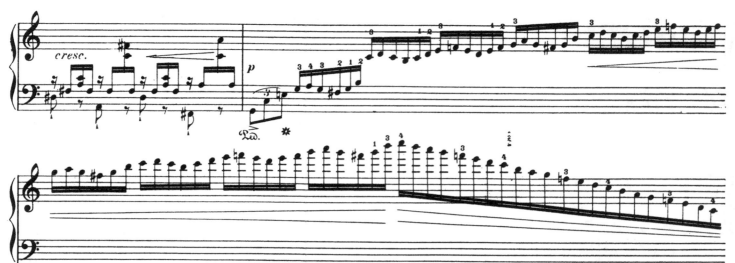

Nº 2.

(1) This "*p*" is borrowed from measure 1 of the First Cadenza.

(2) The superfluous rest (in small print), together with the small notes belonging to it, and the *"dolce,"* are transcribed from the Br. & H. edition. All these (except a forgotten ♭ before *b*) also occur in a copy (Royal Library; formerly Fischhof).

(1) More exactly, according to the principal text:

*)After said copy,
(better):

(2) If this fermata, given in the principal text, be sustained, it must occupy the time-value of five quarter-rests.

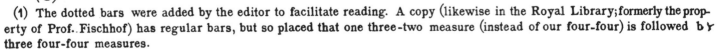

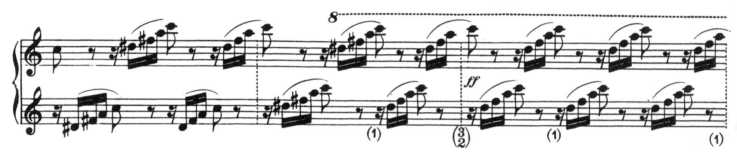

(C)

(1) The above-mentioned copy also has three bars here.

(1) Here Breitkopf & Härtel read [music], which is probably owing to a clerical error; *cf.* the second measure following. The above-mentioned copy reads like Br. & H.

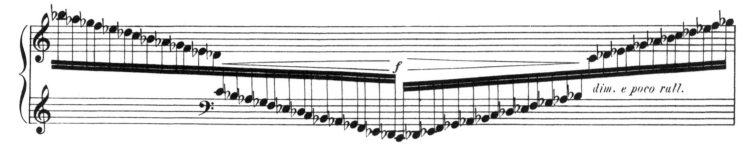

(★) After the aforesaid copy: 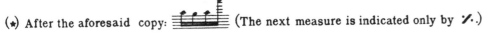 (The next measure is indicated only by ✗.)

(1) This very fine and grandly conceived Cadenza, which seems to have reached its close on this trill, (and, in point of fact, would appear to be quite adequate in length,) again modulates to *G*-major, and (it must be said) in a rather uninteresting and (harmonically) wholly unsatisfactory manner, in order to set off another motive of the Concerto. But remember, that these Cadenzas are unedited works, and that the composer himself applied the file liberally to his works, and sometimes even remodelled them [Th., II, 87]. We therefore suggest to those who find that our by no means irreverent criticisms are justified by the facts, to play, instead of the above measure, the following abbreviated phrase and then to pass over directly to the sign 𝄋 on p. 81, thus preserving the interesting closing passages of the Cadenza.—Or one might—as the traditional closing trill makes a thoroughly characteristic and harmonious impression in the present Concerto—employ the close already derived by the editor from the present Cadenza for the first one:

Page 79, last measure.—When we wrote the first Note on this measure, we had not yet seen the copies of Beethoven Cadenzas in Prof. Fischhof's literary remains. A proof (even if not wholly conclusive) of our conjecture that this passage is not quite correct, is to be found, we think, in a Note to the copy under consideration, according to which there were written into the Autograph, and in pencil (by the composer himself, most likely [?]), a few chords, which we, admittedly, are unable to decipher with certainty, but which, by their very presence, sufficiently indicate the idea of a proposed variant.— We now repeat this passage, as given in this copy:

(1) Here the aforesaid copy reads: etc (?)

(1) At * the oft-mentioned copy has bars; at ** no half-rests and then no arpeggio-sign; and at *** only "*ff*"